101 Things to Do in

VIRGINIA

Before You Up and Die

SWEET WATER PRESS

ISBN: 1-58173-557-X
ISBN-13: 9781581735574

Researched and co-written by Holly Smith
Jacket and text design by Miles G. Parsons
Printed in Italy

1. See Winchester
    in apple
    blossom time.

2. Learn to play the fife.

3. Watch fireworks
over the York River
on the Fourth
of July.

4. See the wild ponies on Assateague.

5. Hike the Blue Ridge.

6. Camp the Blue Ridge.

7. Drive the Blue Ridge.

8. Do anything in the Blue Ridge.

9. Cruise the Potomac.

10. Go surfing at Virginia Beach.

11. See Jamestown.

12. Drive the Chesapeake Bay Bridge-Tunnel.

13. Visit the Virginia Museum of Fine Arts.

14. Tour a winery.

15. Bob for apples.

16. Hike the Appalachian Trail.

17. Go antiquing in Richmond.

18. See the stars from Leander McCormick Observatory.

19. See Williamsburg at Christmas.

20. Explore Ivy Creek.

21. Try the 18th-century cooking at Michie Tavern.

22. Make apple cider.

23. See Thomas Jefferson's grave.

24. Go horseback riding in the Shenandoah Valley.

25. Pay your respects at Arlington National Cemetery.

26. Reenact at Manassas.

27. Tailgate at a NASCAR race.

28. Plant a dogwood.

29. See the Great Stalacpipe Organ in Luray Caverns.

30. Rent a cabin on Big Walker Mountain.

31. Go trout fishing on the Rapidan.

32. Stay at a B&B in the Blue Ridge Highlands.

33. Walk across a
covered bridge.

34. Go apple
picking.

35. Go skydiving.

36. Watch UV and Virginia Tech battle it out.

37. Figure out what really happened to Edgar Allan Poe.

38. Walk in Washington's footsteps, then have dinner at the Mount Vernon Inn.

39. See the grave of Stonewall Jackson's horse.

40. Spend the night in a lighthouse.

41. Tour Bacon's Castle.

42. Visit the aquarium on Chincoteague.

43. Go whale watching.

44. Take a ride in a hot-air balloon.

45. See the world's largest cured ham.

46. Make par.

47. Tour Ash Lawn-Highland, home of James Monroe.

48. See Montpelier, home of James Madison.

49. Stand on the spot where Patrick Henry said, "Give me liberty or give me death!"

50. Go snow skiing.

51. Hike to Cascades Falls.

52. Canoe the New River.

53. Say a prayer at Appomattox.

54. Sail Chesapeake Bay.

55. Visit the Virginia Zoo.

56. Pig out at a chili festival.

57. Indulge at a chocolate festival.

58. Have a boiled peanut eating contest.

59. See a production at Arlington's Signature Theatre.

60. Visit the dinosaurs at the Virginia Museum of Natural History.

61. Spot a famous
politician in
Alexandria.

62. Ride a ferry across the James River.

63. Boat down the Rivanna River.

64. Tour Shenandoah Caverns.

65. Visit Edgar Cayce's Association for Research & Enlightenment.

66. Tour the Berkeley Plantation.

67. Take a riverboat cruise aboard the <u>Annabel Lee</u>.

68. Be an Astronaut for a Minute at the Virginia Air & Space Center.

69. Take a tour of
The Pentagon.

70. See a horse race
at Colonial Downs.

71. Visit the Virginia Holocaust Museum.

72. Catch a hockey game.

73. Explore the Money Museum at the Richmond Fed.

74. Hear the Virginia Symphony Orchestra.

75. Walk along the boardwalk at Cape Charles.

76. See a show at Barter Theatre.

77. Discover the mystery of Mountain Lake.

78. See the Norfolk mermaids.

79. Ride in a horse-drawn carriage.

80. Go fox hunting.

81. See the U.S. Marine Corps Memorial.

82. See a black bear.

83. Kayak the
James River.

84. Learn to clog at the Galax fiddling convention.

85. Tour the USS <u>Wisconsin</u>.

86. Go ice-skating.

87. Take a dolphin cruise.

88. Eat a Virginia ham.

89. Go crazy at
Rockin' Rosie's
Fun House.

90. Ride a roller
coaster at Busch
Gardens.

91. Go deep-sea fishing.

92. Attend a production of the Virginia Shakespeare Festival.

93. Tour Arlington House.

94. Stay at the Martha Washington Inn.

95. Take part in a Revolutionary War reenactment.

96. See John-Boy's bedroom.

97. Save a sea turtle.

98. Master the recipe for homemade biscuits.

99. Saunter down Richmond's Riverfront-Canal Walk.

100. Get a tan on Virginia Beach.

101. Stand on
a mountain and
be glad.
You're in Virginia!